THE ALL-SEEING EYE
COLLECTED POEMS

SHANG QIN

Translated from the Chinese by

JOHN BALCOM

Literature from Taiwan Series
in collaboration with
the National Museum of Taiwan Literature
and National Taiwan Normal University
General Editor: Nikky Lin

CAMBRIA
PRESS

THE ALL-SEEING EYE:
COLLECTED POEMS BY SHANG QIN

Library of Congress CIP data on file.
ISBN 9781621966210

TRANSLATOR'S ACKNOWLEDGEMENTS

I first encountered the poetry of Shang Qin some forty years ago when I was a young student in Taipei. His early prose poems made an immediate and indelible impression. Shang Qin is one of the best poets of his generation, and, for me stands with Lo Fu and Ya Hsien as a triumvirate. I have translated and published collections of poetry by Lo Fu and Ya Hsien and had long wished to do the same for Shang Qin. On one trip to Taipei, I even discussed such a project with the poet and received his permission and blessing. However, due to other obligations over the intervening years, the project never came to fruition. That is until last year when I was unexpectedly contacted by Jade Fu of the Grayhawk Agency about translating a collection of Shang Qin's poetry for Classic Literature, a translation project funded by the National Museum of Taiwan Literature. New life was breathed into an old dream; life comes full circle. I would like to thank Jade Fu and Ping Chang of the Grayhawk Agency for helping to make this book happen.

This translation has benefited from the advice of three people in particular: my wife Yingtsih, Megan Weng, and Anna Holmwood. The dialog with these three careful and sensitive readers sent me back to the originals more than once, deepening my appreciation of Shang Qin's poetry. Their comments and suggestions have improved this translation; any infelicities or errors that remain, I own.

This translation was originally published in a limited edition of twenty-five copies by the National Museum of Taiwan Literature for promotional purposes. I would like to thank the Museum and the Ministry of Culture for funding the translation and for consenting to it being reprinted here. I am grateful to Cambria Press, Toni Tan and David Armstrong in particular, for making this new edition possible. I would also like to express my gratitude to Mr. Tzu-hsien Tung for his generosity in providing a subvention contributing to the publication of this book.

Finally, I would like to dedicate this translation to my wife Yingtsih, with whom I have shared a lifetime of reading and discussing poetry and its translation.

John Balcom is an award-winning translator of Chinese literature, philosophy, and children's books. Dr. Balcom teaches at the Middlebury Institute of International Studies and is a past president of the American Literary Translators Association.

I / *Dream or Dawn*

II / *Dream or Dawn or Others*

III / *Thinking with Our Feet*

IV / *Uncollected Poems*

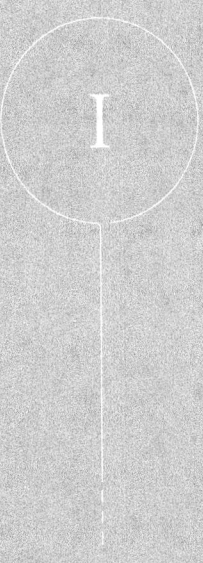

Dream or Dawn

PATH

In March when the nightingale first begins to sing, a night watchman told me about that cosmologist's path, and when I thought about the difficulties he had knocking down that fence during the day, I couldn't help but cry: "You suffer from somnambulism, and so you get up at night to build walls, and yet strangely, you see not your own world...."

SCULPTING

At dusk the color of the wine of happiness and longevity. On the edge of my uneroded forehead, in my eyes, in my ears, I cast my shadow before her, covering her completely.

She is a sculptress. She creates sound in her own auditory canals; and from the very beginning I said: "I come not to cast myself into you, but to leave your hands." However, she molds my bust upside down, oh, upside-down, I then awaken at dawn, and excel dawn.

In memory, her delicate rosy hands have become a pale purple.

THE TURKEY

A child told me when the turkey is about to eat, the flesh on his beak stiffens and stands upright like a horn. My thought was that the turkey is not a gossipy fowl, and when he does make a sound it is only to protest.

Tail feathers spread, the turkey resembles a peacock (even their calls are the same, which I find so very sad). But the peacock flaunts his beauty out of loneliness, while the turkey is always demonstrating against the Void.

The turkey that demonstrates against the Void has no grasp of metaphysics.

He likes to eat the chlorophyll-rich tips of spring onions.

He likes to talk about love, but rarely walks with his love.

He is often thinking, but of things we know nothing about.

"JUMPING GROUND"

At a bend in a mountain road paved with tranquility, an empty cab slowly and unconsciously comes to a stop. The young driver suddenly recalls that this spacious, open turnout is called a "jumping ground." "Yes, jumping ground." Then he thinks of the question of what is up and what is down – he's a little unclear; and then there's the question of rent, "Can the soul also be rented....?"

But when he drives several fares past the place, he suddenly slams on the brakes and weeps, head down over his steering wheel; he thought, have I smashed the car I'm driving that I stopped with me inside.

Note: Jumping ground is a term used by the engineering corps to refer to a turnout at a bend in a mountain road.

GIRAFFES

After the young jailer discovered that at each monthly physical exam the prisoners' necks had grown longer, he reported it to the warden in charge: "Sir, the windows are too high!" but in reply, he was told: "No, they are looking far ahead in time."

The benevolent young jailer didn't know what time looked like, nor did he know where time came from, and he did not know time's whereabouts; so every night he went to the zoo to the giraffe pen to keep watch.

FIRE EXTINGUISHER

Anger flaring at high noon, I stare at the fire extinguisher on the wall. A child walks over and says to me: "Look! There are two fire extinguishers in your eyes." On account of this guileless statement, I cup his face between my hands, and can't help but cry.

I see two mes crying, one in each of his eyes; but he can't tell me how many of him there are reflected in my tears.

PIGEONS

Suddenly I clench my right hand into a fist and drive it violently into the palm of my left hand, "POW!" What desolate wilderness! Then, a flock of pigeons flies through the sickly sky – are they alone or in pairs?

In my left hand, I firmly grip my gradually loosening right hand, my fingers unfold, little by little, but, unable to fully unfurl, they keep turning in my hand. O, innocent hands, you who have worked and will go on working, who have killed and will themselves be killed in the end, now, you resemble a wounded sparrow. And a flock of pigeons flies across the dizzy sky – are they alone or in pairs?

Now, using my left hand, I gently caress my trembling right hand, but my left itself begins to tremble, making it look even more as if it pitied her wounded other half, oh, that grieving bird. So I gently caress my left hand with my right… Perhaps those soaring in the sky are vultures.

There is not one single sparrow in all the bloodless sky. O, innocent hands who depend so upon each other, who tremble, who have worked and will go on working, you hands who have killed and will be killed in the end, now, let me lift you up. How I want to set you free – as if I were releasing a pair of healed sparrows!

TAIPEI, 1960

1

Beside the faltering light of day, in a charcoal mood spying on it as it breathes its last, with rose-colored crêpe paper to kindle the clouds, giving a half-closed window a fine binding; farther out in the suburbs behind a kiln, a lonely look in the eyes scorches the unseen backside of the mountains.

2

On Hengyang Road, the day casts its heart from its chest, alongside the indifferent buildings, it slowly hangs down to remove our quicksilver glasses in order to placate our brief upward-turned daytime glances; the heart's red color is dark and gentle, that immensity reduces it once again to a small insectivorous rodent; we are charcoal made not by kiln-burning ourselves. If someone walks west it is because a cold wind blows from the silver screen; and so brews the desire to smoke and drink.

3

City without fountains; ah, poor setting sun, I praise you with a shower. It has been too long since I spit tears on anyone. As for those four tenacious beasts, their saliva traces for us a hand that can never be retracted.

4

On the revolving gate at New Park, a naughty child in an ant-shooing mood directs the approaching night to enter on this side, the day to exit on the other.

TOY STATION WAGON

—for the younger generation that died young
under the wrinkled pink sky

The children's toy station wagon collided with the glowing leaves and laughter in a field of sorghum that had just started blooming. A huge pack of dreams without dreamers floats in a ditch emitting black bubbles; some of them even show their crooked wheels. Show their handbrakes outside their necks. On that side of the tracks, apparently the end of the road, is the garbage dump.

Tomorrow is covered already by yesterday.

The children's toy station wagon is parked beside the softly flowing stream.

An abandoned dream breaks its zipper on the bridge of a nose.

A lollipop glitters on a smoking canon that is gradually melting.

In a courtyard swept by the wind, beside a chicken coop empty save for a few feathers and some manure, one child, chin in both hands, squats beside an overturned toy station wagon, and sees through the dizzyingly blue sky in a fresh puddle of his own urine on the ground.

AH-LIAN

Ah-lian, if it is night
I can light a thought
In your womb-like warmth and darkness
Illuminating that single stream
Adrift in your soft, fine hair
Fish aswim, with your red tail
You slap the left atrium of my heart
Forcing it to vomit up nearly half of spring
(It was November then)

                                        That was last year

November's counterfeit spring
Secretly moved everywhere
I don't know why I should laugh
If someone cut off your
Street corner, then there'd be two
And spring is elliptical
Winter is being cut again and again

If you hit me with a red pectoral fin
Ah-lian, you'll meet with a hug
Your ears will be bitten

                                (Turn that red handle)

Ah-lian, if there is no night
Daylight will not come, dusk will die
If there is dawn without end
Two pale purple breasts adorned with fish hung dead
Someone's arm will petrify on the pillow
Someone's neck will be carved in relief there
Crystallized salt, and be shattered by a shooting star

Ah-lian, if it is night
The villagers will lift naked bamboo poles and hang up count-
less
Lanterns for peace and happiness and put on sugarcane-leaf hats
Seeing the darkness in the quiet courtyard
Being polished into a dark black gemstone
By the lantern light
My green arms crossed above
And died there. But
Ah-lian, you don't know that someone is watching you in secret
Someone in your belly
Molds new names out of the wind
In your womb-like warmth and darkness

Ah-lian, turn that red handle
Otherwise I'll hear you someplace else
Where folks dye tears pretty colors
Hang strands of them in the doorway to separate
the cold from the warmth
On the iron tail-end of an oil tanker

I hear your terror
Cut off by the shadows cast by the trees
On the pedestrian island, and trampled by sad words
Never again to be hugged, never again to be bitten

Note: Ah-lian is a small village in Kaohsiung County.

GANGSHAN PEAK

Thinking of your countenance among the trees, your trees
I can't recall how the car powdered your face
Looking up at your ashen forehead
Protruding above all the fields
You exhibit indecisiveness
An ox cart passes by
Carrying some seasons, which ones is unclear

Thinking of your morning in the park, your flowers
I recall those soon to ripen fruits
None apparently spontaneous, I wonder
If they haven't taken on a contagious color

Mirroring Gangshan Peak, just one night
I find it hard to bear, hard to bear
Your hot springs are intensely cold
Your breath incredibly hot
Turning the night's cheeks purple
Freezing the luminous beads of sweat

Your spring never coming is hard to bear
Will summer stay forever?

THE FLEEING SKY

the face of the deceased is a marsh never seen by man
the marsh in the wilderness is part of the sky's flight
the fleeing sky is flooded with roses
the overflowing roses are snows that have never fallen
the snows that have never fallen are the tears in the arteries
the welling tears are fiddled fiddle strings
the fiddle strings being fiddled are a burning heart
the cremated heart is the wilderness of marshes

REMOTE HYPNOTISM

On the sickly
Island perhaps it's raining now
Salt is drying on your pillow
Night stands on the other side of salt's window
Night   Night is able to keep watch over you

Keeping watch over the soil keeping watch over the salt
Keeping watch over you   keeping watch over the trees
Because the soil is keeping watch over the trees
Because the trees are able to keep watch over you

Because the trees are able to keep watch over the night
In the forest the birds are able to keep watch over the trees
The birds in the trees are able to keep watch over the stars
The stars in the night are keeping watch over you

Because the stars are able to keep watch over the night
The clouds in the sky are keeping watch over the stars
The clouds among the stars are keeping watch over the wind
The wind in the night is keeping watch over you

Because the wind is able to keep watch over the night
The grass on the land is keeping watch over the wind
The grass in the wind is keeping watch over the dew
The dew in the night is keeping watch over you

Because the dew is able to keep watch over you
Keeping watch over the soil keeping watch over the trees
Keeping watch over the mountain ridge keeping watch over the
mist
The mist in the night is keeping watch over you

The mist in the night is keeping watch over the river
The water in the river is keeping watch over the fish
Keeping watch over the mountain   keeping watch over the
shore
The mountain beside the sea is keeping watch over you

The mountain in the night is keeping watch over you
The mountain in the night is keeping watch over the sea
Keeping watch over the beach keeping watch over the waves
The boat on the waves is keeping watch over you

Keeping watch over the waves keeping watch over the night
Keeping watch over the beach keeping watch over you
Keeping watch over the riverbank keeping watch over the water
I am keeping watch over you in the night

Keeping watch over the mountain ridge keeping watch over the
night
Keeping watch over the soil keeping watch over you
Keeping watch over the stars, keeping watch over the dew
I am keeping watch over you in the night

Keeping watch over the trees keeping watch over you
Keeping watch over the grass keeping watch over the night
Keeping watch over the wind   keeping watch over the mist
I am keeping watch over you in the night

Keeping watch over the voice keeping watch over the night
Keeping watch over the sparrows keeping watch over you
Keeping watch over the war keeping watch over death
I am keeping watch over you in the night

Keeping watch over the forms keeping watch over you
Keeping watch over the speed keeping watch over the night
Keeping watch over the shadows keeping watch over darkness
I am keeping watch over you in the night

Keeping watch over solitude keeping watch over the night
Keeping watch over the distance keeping watch over you
I am keeping watch over the night
I am keeping watch over you in the night

GRADIENT OF THE MILKY WAY

North by northwest in the sky
A flock of sheep are a column of silence
Another form of longing
In another manner
The pasture is east of the Milky Way, then
The pool is within the heart
The heart is in the corpulent guitar

For one night only, the Milky Way
Sets its gradient askew
As if tranquility were knocked askew
And lowers the most important
Leaf toward the water's surface
To meet the stars there

The Milky Way hangs down toward the water's surface
The stars call softly
Countless simple bodies
Moved by their own reflections

The guitar sails on waves of sound
The grassland
Floats under the sails and hawsers
Shedding tears

And being a sister to the pond
Between the high-tension wires and the grape trellises
The Milky Way bends over itself
Directly to my southeast
Caught between two rows of swamp mahoganies
The sound of a dead motor
The moldy
Sigh is midnight's sonic boom
My friend asks the way with cubes of sugar
Lost in the forest beneath the eaves
No one knows the uncertainty you feel watching her wash her hair
At that time, the Milky Way was below the pasture

No one knows the uncertainty I feel when I watch you dry your
hair in the sun
God of the Earth, how boring it is to die
Time seeps from the vegetable basket
To become a beehive
To ferment
The honey sweet only to a blind man's chewing
Since the Milky Way shifted its
Gradient to my flat temples
North by northwest in the sky
There is day and there is night
Night goes, never to return
Day comes, never to depart
March sways between two shoulders

A skirt is burned away by a stare, the body
Melts into a lane of sunshine
Leaving the gradient of the Milky Way
In an empty wine glass.

A TREE AMONG TREES

so happy the tree under the eyelashes
in a sidelong glance, a tree in fog
on earlobe brushed by fog's fingers
earlobe between teeth kissed by the tongue

tree on nose-tip is still
in smelling, tree in the wind
in short moustache flapped by the wind's skirt
short moustache on the lips kissed by nose tip

radiant tree at edge of forehead
in teardrops, tree in rain
on cheeks touched by toes of rain
cheeks by temples kissed by long hair

in eyes   are stars in the fog
in dew,   in trembling
in ears   is a stream in the rain
in wind,   in sobbing

in the hands is fog in the crook of an arm
in the hair is wind between the back and front of the neck
there is rain on a face
there is fog at tip of nose

there is a brook in the valley
there is a road beside the brook
there is a tree in the forest
there is a heart in the tree
in the tree in the tree
among the trees, is a very sad tree

tree among trees
tree between trees
ah, that tree among trees

DREAM OR DAWN

Passing through layers of exhausted cloud   and
Sleepy stars   propping up
Ice-cold temples
Refusing to give into sleep   to
Yawn and stretch   and the wind in the dense forest
A black square-mouthed chimney
            Still belches hot air
The exhaustion of the clouds doesn't count
In the sky there is a dream wounded by a meteorite

(Keep your head and hands inside the window)

The dream was wounded in a weak air current   enwrapping
The destroyed is the meteorite in the end   that pride
Passing through or accompanying the falling mist
But then the constellation that is about to topple
Its icy temples
Leaning on the peak, awake year in and year out
The wind passes over a stretch of camouflage grass
It's difficult for the star-colored dew not to appear on the gray,
gray canon

(Keep your head and hands inside the window)

The star-colored dew is everywhere on the deep green grassland
And even on the balcony   the balcony where water accumu-
lates
On the roof if there's escaping sky
But the dream has crossed the sea
Such a wild wind   passing through
Your bushy hair that rested on the clouds
But my dream
Still on the star-colored grassland
Still being chewed by the ferns of time
Passing through
The tightly shut full view of the eyes

(Keep your head and hands inside the window)

In flight
My dream has all-seeing eyes
The exhausted clouds rise continuously and disperse
The wind glides over the thoughtful lake
In the mountains   the myrtle slowly releases
Its purple
But its voice still hasn't been conferred on an oriole
Unable to strike up
Passing over   the mountain peaks or the luke-warm temples
of the constellation
From a distance, I sense the sophistication of your sobs
Perhaps   the squadron has already set off
(Keep your head and hands inside the window)

Perhaps the ships have already raised anchor
The mist falls in hastiness
Once again you are late
The tide rises
Passing over   the silk tree like a piano keyboard
Unfurling its leaves one after another   passing over the voice

(Keep your head and hands inside the window) passing over

And just on the point of touching the satisfaction of her
Dream (Keep your head and hands inside window)
The acute angle of my dream's dream   encarved
(Keep your head and hands inside the window)
And daily you must come
        Always paving her swollen eyelids
        With the first ray of sunlight
Are you the dawn
I finally surpass and that we
Cook every morning?

DOOR OR SKY

Time: being debated
Place: there is not one iota of sky
          inside the walls with no roof that's
          surrounded by barbed wire that's
          surrounded by a moat without a counterscarp
Character: an unguarded prisoner
               A path
               Tight against the foot of the wall
               Trod out by that jailed prisoner.
The jailed person walking on the path
               finally departs from the path worn by his
Footsteps
He walks to the center of the walled-in area
And cuts down several trees with his hands.

He uses his teeth and his two hands
With the trees and vines he cut down by hands and teeth
Makes a door;
A door with only a door frame is barely a door
(Tie it to a big tree.)

He scrutinizes it carefully for a moment;

He ponders it deeply for a while.

He pushes the door;
He goes out…

He goes out, takes a few steps and turns around
Again, he pushes the door
Out he goes.
Emerges.
Exits.

Under not one iota of sky. Inside the walls with no roof that are surrounded by barbed wire that is surrounded by a moat without a counterscarp on a path tight against the foot of the wall trod out by that unguarded prisoner round a distant center, the unguarded prisoner pushes open a door with door only a door frame that is barely a door that he built with his own hands

And goes out.
Comes out.
Goes out.
Comes out. Goes out. Goes out. Comes out. Comes out. Goes out.
Out. Out. Out. Out. Out. Out. Out.

Until we see the sky.

II

Dream or Dawn or Others

BUS

Stretched by the wind, twisted by the road: the speed blurs the faces on the bus including mine as well as my vexations; I don't know the whereabouts of my feet and even my chronic rheumatism is left behind me. But what I find most incomprehensible is the driver – his woeful temples seem to have some non-mechanical perplexity – how can he see his feet from the windshield filled with scenery; upon arriving at the station the bus stops with the elastic snap of a rubber band; only after getting off the bus do I realize that the driver had placed his two feet on the engine hood, from which point on, he could only sigh: "O, the ambiguity, the ambiguity."

SAFETY ISLAND

1

Getting off the last bus
The passenger steps in a puddle of moonlight
Agitating all the stars in the sky

Why does the safety island pretend to catnap
Trees and the sidewalk and a look of disdain
Emerge from of the depths of our timidity

2

The speeding vehicles and the tilt of the trees
Looks of surprise rush head-on
The waiter who dropped and broke the dishes looks up and
heaves a deep sigh

For your driver the greatest perplexity
Two lines that will never meet

WEEPING OR FORGETTING

Weep for what can't be clearly remembered. Clouds layered high between the brows and a dexterously moving finger. Cloth dolls fully cover the corpse of time on the stairway of ambiguity.

This perhaps is a sort of forgetting. You are the fog on a hill amid low-growing scrub. Who is the misty balcony? Who is the dew? I am the footsteps sounding that year after the war at four in the morning echoing in a long corridor frightening myself.

We are fog. Whether in joy or sorrow, on a marshy delta, among the reeds, we are an unseen boat. The only thing that can be heard is the oars pouring out their hearts, which is two (voice) parts of our song.

If we really weep, scull and oar, sorrowful reeds, we lack – our voices have died in the lobes of our lungs. But our tears fall on the stone balustrade, the bronze incense burner, even though they do not weep.

On a cold night, on the root hairs chewed by a mole cricket and leaves eaten by small grubs. The fog on the ocean rusts the soldier's bayonet, but tears do the job even quicker. Stars and the moon shine alike on places at war and no war.

ANGEL INDULGING IN WINE

After the wine bottle falls and breaks, not only does the drinker sigh for the permeating aroma of the liquid spreading in all directions, but he also prostrates himself and mumbles, "It's not your fault any more than it is mine. Why? Were you careless? Everyone else likes the green heaven, but you disdain the fat, awkward chrysanthemum – to be sure, it really looks foolish – but I can't help you, as I am already a little tipsy." Because an angel is already indulging in his spilled wine – or who knows, maybe it overflowed from a full bottle of wine in another place – its little translucent yellow wings are already dissolving in the pale green liquid...

"Okay." The drinker says, "Be a real man like me." The sound of his voice is so high that it was audible only to a blind old mouse and a baby less than one month old.

WAKING

They daub lime on my face
They drop asphalt over my body
They smear discarded brake fluid on my face and body
They install two blood-red lights for my eyes
They insert gear wheels in my mouth
They shine a spotlight on me
They hide in a dark place
They keep watch on me with their rodent eyes
They record the tossings of my body

Out through an orifice it goes. My soul.

Having met with all sorts of desires, fears and sorrows by chance, my soul returns from a dream of visiting a house of pleasure in the busy downtown, and catches sight of my own body, which has been made into something no longer in a human form lying on the bed; as expected, at first, I was stunned by their mischief; and then, though I was run through with a sharp blade, my own hands could not deter me. My soul drifted over like the permeating fragrance of flowers through the window, drifted over and now tightly embraces this stinking bag of flesh, soaked in the familiar sweat of a nightmare, for together they have been looking after each other for nearly forty years, as working children, as vagabonds; when they were truant together hanging happiness on the tree, "Come, wind! Come, wind!" when they deserted their posts together carrying fear on new grass sandals with broken heels. They fell down together, got up together, refused to cry and refused to shout in pain! They also fell in love. When they were angry, they silently struck at the wind, striking their own palms with their fists, nearly risking their lives.

A BLACK CRYSTAL WITHOUT SUBSTANCE

"We should turn out the lights before undressing; otherwise, the 'light' will remain on our skin."

"Because it is persistent?"

"Because it is a kind of insulator."

"Then, what about the moon?"

"It's the same as the starlight." The bed curtains are lowered after the lights are turned out and all that remains outside is the stiff night. After the hair of the people inside the room disappears, and then their lips and tongues vanish, followed by the disappearance of their embracing hands and arms, shoulders, and chests. Their legs and ankles vanished a little later, after which it is the turn of so-called 'existence.'

N'etre pas. They weren't really dissolved by the darkness; but rather they joined and purified the darkness, used it; "O, it's so difficult to create a black crystal without qualities."

LITTLE BROTHER AMOEBA

A child tugs on a corner of my grass-green garment, the little amoeba brother wails and rails, retreating down the stairs. After much vacillation, I refuse his invitation. This is simply a beast howling at the moon. His neck says: Why not come upstairs to my home? It is then that you notice the ladder, long and narrow. Do you have a nest and some stars in the city?

I find it strange that someone has such a brother. "Is he both clean and dirty?" He is like a raccoon's paw, the palm of which I think must be like the front claws of a pangolin. A person with an amoeba for a little brother resembles both a raccoon and a pangolin, while I, on the streets late at night, walk with several dozen shadows.

A FROZEN TORCH

Late at night, the electricity went out. Hunger followed the attack of darkness. I lit a candle and went to the fridge to find something to eat. At precisely the same time I opened the refrigerator and found what I wanted, I suddenly discovered that the candlelight, the carnelian-red flame, and the smoke like long black hair, had, alas! All frozen. Just like when you open your heart and discover therein, a frozen torch.

LADDER

Not more than twenty-five meters from the window in front of my desk is small flat-roofed concrete building; it used to be a garage, but has since been abandoned. Last winter, someone leaned a bamboo ladder, which was a third taller than the building, against it.

Outside my window are a number of small cherry trees. In the winter, I can see the water stains and cracks in the wall of the building through their thin, naked limbs; recalling the vestiges of existence. Spring comes quickly on the heels of winter. The white blossoms of the cherry trees in full bloom and their quick passing have never disturbed me. And suddenly summer arrives.

One afternoon, I was sitting at my desk, bored stiff. I put my hands on the edge of the desk and leaned back. At that moment a scene suddenly appeared to me; after the cherry trees were covered with a dense canopy of leaves I could no longer see the water stains and cracks on the little building. I could only look over the tops of the trees, O, all I could see was that the ladder was still there, the part that was higher than the roof jutting up into the sky. The sky was as blue as the ocean; at that moment a piece of cloud just like the patch of a sail slowly sailed from the end of the ladder. At the same time, a thought rose in my mind, and I said, "The devil only knows! How could I have such an absurd thought?" As I was berating myself, Mr. Chen was standing behind me and said:

"What's the matter? Who are you thinking about?"

"The devil only knows!" As I spoke, I pointed at the ladder and the cloud, "Hey, look." Right then, the ladder started to shift— someone must have been moving it.

"Wait! Wait!" He shouted madly. With total disregard for all else, he stepped across my desk, rushed through the window, and fell to the ground, where he kept shouting madly: "Wai...t! Wai...t!" But all I could do was to bend over my desk submissively and sigh.

GLOVES

Once, after I finished work, I returned to my bedroom, took off one of my gloves and tossed it on the bed; I then took out a cigarette and placed it between my lips and just as I'd struck a match and was about to inhale, I looked over at the glove through the floating black smoke from the tip of the flame. The coarse white glove lying on the bed had been turned yellow by the yellow soil, and had been turned black by black soil, and having been stained by the yellow soil and the black soil it had now turned a reddish brown.

At that moment the glove was naturally empty, having been parted from my hand; the forefinger was bent at a thirty-degree angle, the little finger was pressed under the ring and middle fingers, and could not be seen, appearing to have been cut off. O, how full of loneliness and sadness it was. I hurriedly extinguished the match and threw it away, removed the other glove, and dropped it beside the other.

The second glove lay supine. Its fingers lost the strength to spread, the tips pointing at the other glove from a distance of ten centimeters, forming a right angle. You could say it was resting, but it seemed to tremble; in this way, a single reddish-brown coarse white glove was more symbolic than anything else; hope without hope, an absolute and empty sadness, like ten million dispirited souls. As though it were a widower in a suit, dancing a slow waltz.

JOKE

I once played a big joke on a group of ants.

Just after a summer downpour, the air was particularly fresh. A group of ants was building a new den. Every ant carried a grain of yellow soil from out of the hole, depositing it a centimeter and a half away; and those minute grains of yellow soil quickly piled into a small enclosing wall. They all seemed quite happy. Until, that is, I played a big joke on them.

I captured an ant that had gone out in search of food and gently crushed it to death between my fingers; then I dropped it from above their nest; I dropped it in the center of that enclosing wall among the ants who were celebrating their conquest of their territory. I watched those ants, famous for their courage and unity, suddenly become very cowardly and selfish; in less than a second, they had all fled.

III

Thinking with Our Feet

ELECTRIC LOCK

Tonight, the streetlights in my neighborhood went out again right on time at midnight.

As I fumbled for the key, a kind-hearted cab driver shone his bright headlights on me as he was backing up, mercilessly casting my middle-aged shadow on the steel door until I was able to select the right key from my keychain to insert into my heart, after which the kind-hearted cab driver left.

Finally, I gently turned the key in my heart and listened for the click. Then I pulled the deft piece of metal from my heart, opened the door and stepped firmly inside.

I soon grew accustomed to the dark.

THE SPEED OF SOUND

—in memory of Wang Yingxian

Someone jumped off the bridge.

That body, rigid yet flailing chaotically, as if a prop in a movie, suddenly froze in midair for half a second before slowly continuing its fall. It turned out that the sad scream released as he leapt, was bounced back on the water's surface and buoyed him up in midair, so that the final plunge was accompanied by merely one heartbreaking splash.

THE FIRST SEVEN DAYS
AFTER HER DEATH
—in memory of
my daughters' maternal grandmother

They'll all be home soon.

She leans over the river where she washed clothes as a young girl as she was accustomed to do a half century ago, and discovers that she can't lift an ounce of fresh coolness with her hands, moreover the water's surface, as smooth as a mirror, does not reflect her; this reminds her that her daughters-in-law all want to church, but none recite scripture for her nor does she even have a spirit tablet.

A petal from a peach blossom falls from the crescent moon, and grandmother nearly cries. She has almost forgotten that she returned by treading over waves of cogon grass, waves of reed catkins, the waves of the Taiwan Strait, and the waves of Tungting Lake.

THE THIRTY FIVE DAYS
AFTER HIS DEATH
—in memory of
the grandchildren's maternal grandfather

After listening to the subordinates under his command who departed years before him and who today are still wandering, solitary souls complain that all the gods, big or small, have made things difficult for them because they are unable to completely take back the traces of their lifetime, he can't help but heave a sigh on account of the fact that the spirit world is so snobbish. Otherwise, why could he enter the courtyard of his old home unhindered?

But his adjutant used to have another explanation. He said: Sir, the difficulty my soul is having to return home has nothing to do with my rank, rather the problem was the warhead between my legs; although during life, an ache of a different degree allowed me to predict the weather, now I'm not allowed into my house by the door gods because they see me as possessing a dangerous weapon.

Now he finally understands why his daughters-in-law by having him cremated were not disobedient or unfilial. He recalls that when collecting his bones one grandchild mistook the pieces of melted shrapnel next to his spine for medals.

MOURNING FOR MY OLD PLACE
IN A CERTAIN LANE ON A CERTAIN DAY

After dusk
the steel bars project horizontally amongst the rubble
unfold   a copy book of
wildly scribbled steel
dissolving into the subdued blackness
An excavator
crouches in the living room
its single arm reaching
into the kitchen
(it is time to eat)
its arm drips with machine oil
a section of stainless steel skeleton
Whiter than old Heaven
in the corner
is a broken medicine jar
that still holds
the landlord's cough

SILENT CLOTHES

—See washing girl at night,
1980 autumn, Three Gorges.

a girl like moonlight
at water's edge
silently
pounds a hard, black stone

(no one knows to what angle her man drifted)

a girl like reed flowers
by the riverside
silently
pounds the cold, white moonlight

(no one knows to what angle her man wandered)

a girl as cold as moonlight
a girl as white as reed flowers
on the riverside silently pounds
the silent clothes at water's edge

(the dusky distant mountain always shouts in pain after passing)

Note: In the autumn of 1960, I traveled with my poet Fried Liu Sha down the Three Gorges. We stayed in a hotel on a back street by the river in a room built on stilts and half suspended over the river, the water and wind flowing below. We drank rice wine until we were drunk and then went to bed. I was awakened at night by the sound of beating clothes, I pushed aside the window covering, and looked out and saw the moonlight, reed flowers, and the shimmering water, a stretch of clear brightness. The sound of a woman washing clothes by the riverside broke the all-encompassing silence. The pounding of her clothes echoed on the mountains, and it was an unbearably sorrowful sound. Recalling the happiness of my childhood when I accompanied some aunties who washed clothes by the riverside, the splashing water, laughter and chit-chat seemed like only yesterday, I couldn't help but feel sad. I tried to awaken Liu Sha to drink some more, but to no avail, so I drank alone and tried to come up with some lines of verse, but couldn't. I thus spent a restless night. Later, I got drunk with Xiu Tao and some others in the same place, but didn't hear the sound of beating clothes, and again failed to write a single line of verse. Although now, twenty years later, a poem is written, my old friends are scattered. I couldn't help but think of the past and record it.

THINKING WITH OUR FEET

we can't find our feet   on the ground
in the sky   we can't find our heads
we walk with our heads   think with our feet
a rainbow   garbage
is a bridge of nothingness   is a helter-skelter of topics
clouds   a trap
are misty roads   is a foregone conclusion
in the sky   we can't find our heads
we can't find our feet   on the ground
we walk with our heads   we think with our feet.

THE MOSQUITO

After a colleague of mine got married, I took over the little log cabin he built by the river, which also meant taking over a room full of mosquitoes.

Since I replaced the old wood-barred windows with screens, I have missed the pleasure of mistaking the human shadow under the lamplight for a little dog.

In order to banish these buzzing sentient beings from my first very own kingdom, I immediately added a screen door.

But a door must always be opened.

And so it was that finally some uninvited guests took the opportunity of stealing in, despite my being ever so careful, and just one was enough to disturb my peace. However, what really bothered me wasn't its buzzing or that it bit me, but the fact that I don't have it in my heart to tolerate others. The moment I felt the existence of another creature in my room, I found it impossible to calm down to write, to read, or even to think. When trying to kill it with a book or clothes proved ineffective, and I lost track of it, all I could do was calm myself and wait for it to reappear. Seeing it with extreme difficulty as it crawled on the screen door, I thought, since you want out, I'll let you go. But, the moment I went to open the door, it flew back into some dark corner of the room.

How hateful! My hatred began to torment me.

So, I came up with an insidious plan; taking off all my clothes except my underpants, and knowing that mosquitoes don't particularly like bright light, I moved my stool some distance away from the lamp, but where I could still see things clearly; I sat profoundly still and said, "Here, come and get it." I thought, isn't the mosquito the kind of 'person' to stand on ceremony?

Actually I was wrong. While the mosquito doesn't understand human speech, it is no stickler, if it hadn't been for my recent exertion, which left my skin salty with sweat, it would never have been there at all. I think someone once said: the bodies of people who harbor feelings of hatred produce a particularly foul odor.

And mosquitos pursue what is rancid.

It finally came, quietly and by surprise. But it didn't stop where I wanted it to; then the calf of my leg hurt and my skin palpitated, but by the time I moved my leg, it had already flown away.

It was so upsetting, the more I had to retrain myself; and it also reminded me: the mosquito always bites in a dark and hidden place. I continuously flexed my feet and slightly waved my right hand. Finally, with no other choice, it circled and landed on my motionless left arm.

"Alright!" I'm not sure, but perhaps it heard my silent shout of joy, for it once attempted to fly away and, even though it did land again, it still seemed to harbor some suspicion and fear. I kept telling myself that I had to exercise self-restraint and be patient, making an effort to hold my breath. Seeming to have attained my trust, it even took a couple of steps in the sparse fine hair on my arm. Of course I knew it was looking for the best place to bite.

I had felt a slight pain on my skin and could see where its sharp proboscis penetrated skin. First the antennae on either side of its proboscis moved slightly. Clearly its proboscis penetrated even deeper because it could no longer be seen, and only its antennae remaining visible.

It was the sort of mosquito we commonly see in homes, but the kind that grows in vegetation and not in smelly ditches; it was relatively larger and different from the delicate, striped ones in the mountains; simply stated, it was exquisitely formed, with its wings, gray and shiny, spread neatly across its back.

To say that it was exquisitely formed is in no way an exaggeration. Its abdomen was flat and long without being scrawny, and it had alternating black and white stripes. Most beautiful of all were its six slender legs, each of which was about twice as long as its body, and according to the degree of thickness divided into three segments; when it stood on its four front legs, they were evenly placed; while the curve and slope of its legs gave a smooth and steady impression, in conformity with mechanical principles.

The most wonderful thing, though, were its two hind legs, which at that moment were elevated, the height increasing to match the increasing depth to which its proboscis penetrated, causing its rear to be fully elevated, its body at a beautiful fifteen-degree angle to my skin. Or perhaps because when it was sucking blood it needed to exert more force so that its hind legs twitched rhythmically.

And so, the distinct black and white stripes on its abdomen began to expand and grow more indistinct. Actually, all I saw was just the expansion of those black and white stripes, with the black ones first becoming red and the white ones becoming slightly pink. I continued to restrain myself and forced myself to be patient.

Good! You've already sucked my blood into your stomach.

The situation was reminiscent of having one's blood drawn in the military. When the nurse sticks the needle in the vein in your wrist, he asks you if it hurts as you watch the gradations of the syringe fill with fresh red blood. What's different is that drawing blood is a 'business' but for a mosquito to suck blood into its stomach is not just considered a 'business'. I'm sure you won't understand this. I had a vague impression that this really is some transaction of life. Unfortunately, this noble sentiment couldn't be maintained for very long. When the stripes on the mosquito's abdomen vanished entirely and it turned red, and after I felt that it had drunk to its heart's content and was thoroughly intoxicated, I could almost hear the malignant laugher in my heart.

Really, the mosquito was drunk, drunk after drinking human blood.

Its rotund abdomen was not just red, but actually glowed faintly under the light. It really was drunk. Not only had its highly elevated hind legs stopped twitching, but hung there somewhat limply; however, it hadn't yet decided to leave after drinking its fill. It really was drunk. It was perfect.

Under such circumstances, a human being like myself, who is ten thousand times larger than a mosquito, didn't have to consider slapping it at all. I slowly lifted my right hand and extended one finger, my forefinger, and lightly pressed down on its body, pausing briefly, not only to feel its turgidity, but also the warmth of my own blood inside it.

When I moved my finger away, it was not moving. Its proboscis was still deeply embedded in my skin. The fellow couldn't help being greedy but also over-indulging itself. I'm not entirely sure why I didn't forcefully crush its belly; maybe I didn't want to stain my hand with blood or was I afraid to see that the mosquito's blood was my own, or some other reason.

Anyway, it wasn't yet dead, just fainted.

I picked it up between my thumb and forefinger and placed it in my open palm.

I really felt a bit sorry for it, as it clearly had fallen into my trap.

If it were to revive, was I to let it go?

I began to have some regrets: feeding a mosquito with human blood filled with hate. If it went and bit someone else, would it transmit the hate? Would its offspring, if it had any, also be able to transmit hate to other human beings? Of course, this was sheer nonsense. The most reasonable explanation was perhaps that even if I were filled with hate, and my blood was sucked by another life, wouldn't it vanish?

Well, in the end, I didn't let it go. I promptly folded a ball out of paper and placed it inside. Frankly, even if hate can be contagious, is it likely that humanity has always been short of this kind of emotion? As for inheriting, a mosquito doesn't hate, and yet it still sucks blood!

But what really worried me was 'tragic self-awareness', I was afraid lest this trait unique to human beings be contagious to insects.

SKETCHES OF THE FIVE ORGANS

Mouth

How best to put it?

Only that
Eating is of first priority
Songs
It occasionally sings
And it has kissed
Quite a few
Ah – wine bottles

Eyebrows

They are birds with wings only
No bodies

Soaring between
A tear and a smile

Nose

A grave of
Two holes
Without gravestones
Liang Shanbo and Zhu Yingtai
Buried here

Eyes

A pair of fish in love
The tails only appear after forty

The bridge of a nose in between
(like me and my family
A strait in between)
Unable to see each other in this lifetime
Occasionally
We mix
Just their tears in my dreams

Ears

Without the help of two hands
This existence is actually a kind of having no alternative

But then go ahead please
Curse or praise
If someone cuts a fart
The stink
Is a matter for the nose only

Uncollected Poems

A SIGN AT THE BUS STOP

It's simply crazy! Why would they paint the sign at the bus stop the color of papaya? I couldn't help thinking about that upon arriving at the bus stop. Perhaps only the round signs at the suburban stops were done in this way. Otherwise there is a poet in the maintenance department.

After all, not one of the buses that come and go are the one a person awaits and the one awaited never comes. All I can do is lean my exhausted body against the sign, close my eyes and imagine the appearance of a brand-new, empty rainbow-colored bus.

I don't know why the sign drops lower and lower and gradually vanishes and my body sinks along with it, ever downward until my back nearly touches the horizon and my beautiful daughter finally comes and helps me to my feet and says, "Papa, the sun has already set."

CUCKOO

(A girl with two eyes like moons pours a cup of starlight onto the hill of my face, and I awaken.)

On a road covered with plantain, a cliff covers my head with the cry of the cuckoo in its steepness, and I awaken. I hear another cuckoo cry: Return! Return!! Return!!!

Return? I just returned from snot-nosed childhood. The creek has become a road. Paper streamers flutter at the ancestral graves, attracting the departed souls. Awake, I go back and forth and again in dream I go back and forth, returning.

The cuckoo keeps calling: changing to a *shang* tone then a *zhi*; its cry keeps rising, higher and farther away until it is swept away by the drifting clouds.

THE SUNLIGHT ON THE BACKSIDE
OF THE EARTH

The phone rings
In the voice is sunlight from the backside of the earth
And we sit in its shadow
Gazing up at the arrhythmia of Scorpio
Orion tiptoes across the universe
No one sees the three bright stars of his belt
On the backside of the earth

In the ringing of the phone is a grassland
A grasshopper is blown over twelve miles
A taxi at the mouth of an alley scares a cat
Ripping open a garbage bag for something to eat
In the city where I live
There are some yellowed photos crossed by tire tracks

On the backside of the earth is a phone
Spreading cold sunlight
The temperature falls ever lower
Placing an icy hand on
A shoulder like a revolving record gradually slowing
The digitized sound lingering after the electricity goes out
The tardy and messy image of a mosaic

In the shining candlelight blossoming on the burning wick
Flashing eyes
Doubt the phone ever really rang

SPRING

—in memory of Qin Zihao

The first time I saw this clear spring bubbling up, a bamboo dipper appeared in my mind. Why didn't they place one beside the spring? One made out of wood or a gourd would be fine, so people don't have to bend over to taste the clear, cold poetry. I bend over.

When I scoop up the spring water in my two hands, the poet's upside-down reflection looks back at me. I know he still has not returned to his home in the motherland. Nor did he ever go to Taiwan. His relatives at home provided him with a large granite body. He was only twenty years old. The clear, cold spring water has already slipped between my fingers.

I stand up straight, and the poet stands up again. In my twenties – that's how old I was when I met him. When I bid farewell to him at the crematorium, he was fifty-one. Later, his friends gave him a bronze skull.

I bend over again. Faces continue to float up out of the spring water, each one younger than the last. Quickly, I cup them one after another in my hands and splash them on my face: sixty, fifty-five, fifty, forty-five, forty, thirty-five, thirty, twenty-five, twenty-three, twenty-two, twenty-one....

Note: A couple of years ago when I went home for a visit, I took the opportunity to go to Qin Zihao's hometown of Guanghan to pay my respects at the Qin Zihao Memorial Hall. The memorial hall is a traditional style wooden building located in a corner of Fanghu Park. Though the space is small, it is secluded and quiet. In front of the memorial hall is a lotus pond; to the left is the granite statue of Qin Zihao; to the right, a number of mountain stones are piled and out of the cracks between them pours the clear, cold spring water. Anyone who sees it will think of a dipper.

The stone sculpture was perhaps based on a photo of the poet in his youth. He supports his chin with his left hand, which makes him look a little like the Thinker, but his eyes look straight ahead, his bushy brows are slightly knit, giving one the impression of a martyr. Alas, Qin Zihao passed away thirty years ago. At one time I agreed to write an article about his poetry but never completed it. I did finish this poem in his memory, however, which is, I believe, far more appropriate than any theoretical article would be.

A BIG FULL STOP

—laughing in memory of Huang Huacheng

Huang Huacheng, born in a certain month and year

      in his ancestral home someplace in

Guangdong, never once did you mention you did Komeno-style paintings and

wrote fiction   drama   and made short films

wrote "Setting" with rice wine at the theater to fill in for type

failing to be a "Prophet", you took to "Waiting for Godot" without result.

you established your own school of painting, calling Great Taipei Deconstructionism

the discovery of the coolest of cool pop art

your designs incorporated square outsides and round insides or non-round

outsides playing twelve or thirteen tiles at Mahjong no matter what

the enemy was at the table with a spy always beside you

always arriving late and carrying three or four packs of cigarettes on you

you always looked at people over the top of your reading glasses or

the Devil but of angels you were a nonbeliever

in short, he didn't believe in angels or in demons

he put bullets in a baby bottle to feed whose "son of man" whose

dream or dawn did he tear up and paste back together again

as a result two people met in court where he kept yawning

right now he doesn't know which hall he has arrived at since a certain

day in May he quietly left, he should have ridden a bamboo

horse not entirely like the ones he drew

the king of hell that fella surely invited him to have a seat beside him to watch and said Brother

you got the wrong place Godot isn't here he must not have

had any memory-erasing soup and he remembered very clearly and continued smoking

making the fat official cough and the little devil excused himself to take a leak

not paying attention, he walked to the home-viewing terrace and carelessly observed a crowd of friends standing in front of the photo of him, several decades old

coldly he said don't cry or you'll suddenly lose weight

so speaking he lifted his big head and like a balloon hit the Gate of

Heaven startling Sun Wukong who dodged to one side

while all we did was sit on the ground look up and, pointing at this and pointing at that

saying that the ring of light above his head was one big full stop

Note: Huang Huacheng left, casual and refined. He forbade anyone to write an obituary for him or offer him floral wreaths or any such nonsense. Aside from a few relatives who arranged for a memorial service at the crematorium, his friends decided to pay their respects by looking at his thirty-year-old stage photos before saying, let's go!

AESTHETICS OF HEIGHT

—in memory of Mei Xin

He always wrote long, long lines of verse as long as the Yangtze
and Yellow Rivers
He always worked long, long hours as long as the Great Wall
He always urged his friends with long, long sighs
He also drew out his melancholy after smiling as his shadow is
long when he was alone
And now suddenly he rose high, high as the moon and stars and
even farther than
The constellations he used to talk about, as a result he could not
hear us calling...
(Outer space cannot find your tall branches
The fruit you scattered in the stratosphere must be cold and
white)

Note: This is a line from my poem "Tree", which Mei Xin liked very much. Mei Xin was tall, over six feet tall, and was, of course, considered tall among the poets of his generation.

CHICKEN

Sunday, and I'm sitting in a quiet corner of the park on an iron bench missing a leg, enjoying the lunch I got from a fast-food place. Gnawing away at it, I suddenly realize that it has been decades since I last heard a cock crow.

I try to assemble the bones into a domestic fowl that can call to the sun. I cannot find its vocal cords. Because they no longer need to call. Their only job is to eat all the time, and to produce themselves.

Under man-made sunlight
There is neither dream
Nor dawn

EAVES

This is a night job. The first jack hammer starts to work under the streetlights, when the winged beasts slip into the afterglow of sunset. The old house is demolished.

The bats return and circle several times around the excavator in the living room, where so-called eaves no longer exist. One of the bats lands on my gradually shrinking shadow, the sun slowly rises, I move, and it too crawls.

REBEL AND FLEE

When I realize that my numerous shadows actually disregard my coming to a halt and each hides from the light source quietly slinking, I am stunned.

I raise both hands up high, they lower their heads and flee on. I shout and they vanish directly into different dark alleys.

I scream in fear.

SNOW

I fold a sheet of letter paper from the reverse side. It's whiter that way and fortunately he doesn't like to write on both sides. I fold it and fold it again, then fold it diagonally in the shape of a cone. Then I cut it with a small pair of scissors, cut and dig, then

I always think incorrectly that's how snow is made: spread out the cut letter paper, fortunately that person's writing does not show through, white and spread out, six bundles of snowflakes rest on the waxy-yellow palm of my hand. However

At three thousand meters or higher up in the sky, a group of angels faces a pandemonium of bodies on a public square down in the world below and are at a loss as to what to do when the temperature suddenly drops to minus zero, and their arguments and sighs gradually crystallize and float down from the sky.

RAILROAD CROSSING

The crossing bell sounds as the train comes. My daughter, who I am holding in my arms, struggles to turn around. The roar of the train drowns out the *dang*, *dang* of the crossing bell. The red eyes blink continuously. My daughter's gaze is carried away by the train. But she doesn't even know what faraway is.

At the same time my eyesight is frozen because the city – its breathing, air, noise, and crying, has suddenly – has been cut in half until the gate at the crossing rises. But still, I feel nostalgia for the city's other half.

STONE

There's no need to go around and even less need to curse. I once considered sitting upon its belly covered with roots and singing. It never happened. I said, "Hey, not even I would hear it."

After a typhoon passed, a boulder came down, lying face up in the middle of the road allowing me to see a side of it that had never seen the light of day in millions of years. Such a rare opportunity. But I've always been one to take my own road, so, with my usual pace and setting my sights, I headed on until I arrived at a thatched hut halfway up the mountain, and only then did I formally say, "Hello." Just then, the stone was moving someplace internal, growing ever smaller.

PAULOWNIA BLOSSOMS

The paulownia tree grows on a cliff, and the flowers that fall from its branches take a relatively long time to reach the ground; the petals folded to the left spin counter clockwise, round and round and round as they fall; looking up, the people spin clockwise, round and round and round, the sky feels dizzy.

The flowers gradually fall, time revolves slowly. Before the base of each flower hits the ground, many things have happened on Earth. I, for one, have coughed a number of times, promised offerings to a deity for a blessing, and aged many years.

SALTED DUCK EGG

On a log table on which the wood grain is clear to the eye
A salted duck egg nearly blue in color
Lusterless   almost green
A tiny brown ant climbs
On the gray elliptical shadow of the egg

The iron door bangs
Someone   goes for a stroll

AQUARIUM

When I was locked up next to the tropical fish tank, where were you? You forgot your eyes. You left with the employees. Your eyes are in the fish tank. Your eyes swim among the aquatic plants. My eyes patrol in the dark; your eyes are behind the fake hills in the fish tank; my eyes crossed a little bridge between them. You left. Your eyes are still in the tropical fish tank in the aquarium. In my eyes are also fake hills, aquatic plants, and a little bridge. I can stand on top of a little pagoda and shout: Where is the owner of these eyes that can still convey warmth in the dark, the one with long black hair, and a tiny nose!

Next to a tropical fish tank in the aquarium where the employees have turned out the lights and left, a forgotten tourist, gave his eyes to the fish to eat.

SILENT THUNDER

—on a certain day in a certain month
and a certain year,
I attended a show by the painter Chen Tingshi
and conversed with him through writing.

A silent thunderbolt breaks the deep, dark night; the lightning flash races over the bagasse board which has lost all its sweetness. The sun shouts; the sky screams. No one hears a thing except the steel standing in the atrium, except for the iron bars and the rusty lock. And these wild metallic cursive scribbles also shout and sing. Who hears it?

Under the gaze of the cold metal and the warm colors, someone debates at a high decibel on a piece of paper. Silence in a major key.

HE THINKS, THEREFORE HE IS NOT

—for Chu Ge

he brushes the snow and ice from the poet's body
he forces the plum blossoms in the poet's heart to flower
he is a plum blossom
is he ice and snow or warmth
he gently transplants a tree to a
painting he softly calls the mountains' names
he makes the mountains hug and kiss each other
like the hugs and kisses of lovers   the flowers blossom
a flower forgets the leaves he sings
a silent song that carries off flowers, leaves, men and
women to a place in his memory to burn
and consume a row of teeth and a shock of hair
Burning up everything and then thinking
(he thinks, therefore he is not)
and then forgets
forgets poetry and women forgets himself
forgets forgetting

COLORFUL DISTURBANCE

—sketch of Li Xiqi

a barrage of artillery fire roared above from his childhood
his trembling sketch for the aroma of strong liquor
he strides with red-hot steps
he tightly clasps a handful of spun silk
he turns a rotar
he constructs a city
he casts a six-sided fate
he knocks over a domino
under his brushes the colors grow restless
the moon is on his line of peaks
singing a love song to a variable melody
a voice bright as gold lacquer
like the sun behind a storm cloud
like the changes before the arrival of a storm
one stroke of sadness, one of joy
sometimes dry, sometimes scorched, sometimes pale
sometimes heavy
colors restless in his mind

SLASHED OPEN

—sketch of Zhu Weibai

He slashes at the white canvas with a gentle sharpness, numerous strands of metallic light are reflected in his eyes, where crystalline cold meets genial warmth. The air hastily yields. He steadfastly continues to cut. Some fibers in the canvas finally take leave, saying goodbye with a sigh; the air begins to move as the canvas is rolled up, the fragrance of foreign cotton wafts on the wind, shapes like wisps of clouds, cotton fluff, a flock of sheep, and the island surge forth one after another.

Afterwards, the clouds are piled high or it storms
Having been slashed open, space proliferates

THE SIXTH PATRIARCH TALKS
ABOUT PAINTING

—for Xia Yang

A crowd stands in front of a painting, engaged in an endless debate. They shake their heads, sigh, and thump their chests because, while the background is clear and well defined, the people in the painting appear blurred, "Look at the moss on the ancient bricks behind him" "You can almost smell the piss at the foot of the wall" "Is that guy the only one hailing a cab?" "His hand and head are fuzzy like an apparition" "The painting copied from a photograph" "The person in the painting moves" "**The wind moves**" "The camera moves" "**The banner moves**" "The painter's hand moves." "**The mind moves**" it's hard to tell who's speaking. The painter listens for a while then walks off, by himself.

WINDOW IN THE CHEST

—after seeing Luo Zhen's 1997 exhibition

The people of the Country of Piercechest, have holes through
their chests.

—— from *The Classic of Mountains and Seas,*
"The Classic of the Region beyond the Seas: The South"

clouds pass though his chest
on the border between day and night
dreams pass through her chest
there is laughter   there is sobbing
clouds pass between her two breasts
between the crack of sobbing and laugher
dreams pass through the lower part of his deltoid muscle
those wearing smiles, to which quiet sobbing is stuck, all with a
masterless style
all kinds of dreams, big and small, slowly pass through
what are now irregular windows in these bodies of purity
where once were situated heart, lungs and liver.

the next stop is the blue sky.

DREAMING OF OPENING THE LOCKS
IN PAINTINGS

—on seeing Pan Lihong's "1997 Obstructions Series"

No one knows what's behind the doors, no one knows, and besides, they're all locked, different locks for different doors. What is locked behind the doors? They cannot be opened. They are doors in the paintings, they are locks.

What is really locked behind the doors in the paintings? A chain of laughter? A doll that wiped away its tears? An unopened love letter? Jelly made by the moon? Even the painter would like to know.

Every night she dreams of entering a different one of her paintings to open a lock, but each time she forgets to bring the key or brings the wrong one. But by the time she realizes this, the alarm clock goes off. No one will ever know what is locked behind those doors.

FLYING FISH

—for the painter Feng Zhongrui

Did he make a mistake when composing this picture? He pointed the fish's head toward a window in the painting. Who knows, perhaps there is a ladder outside.

When the painter went to sleep, the fish departed without leaving a word. Leisurely and carefree, it left through the oil paints, through the window with the curtains curled by a breeze blowing in the painting. Its fins were wings.

Later, many years later, the fish returned through the mountains in an ink painting. At a fisherman's wharf in a foreign land as a fine rain was falling.

Afterword: Feng Zhongrui was a member of the Four Seas Society and later a member of the May Painting Society. His early oil paintings were Surrealist. He once presented me a painting with a fish. He wandered about and I lost track of his whereabouts, which was regrettable. Zhongrui is now living in the United States and I don't know if he is still painting abstract ink paintings. I miss him very much.

FLYING GARBAGE

The wind whips up.

First it is an old newspaper, yesterday's news, today's history, that is blown over, sent across the street to be trampled again; then comes a plastic bag with light red stripes, nearly transparent, which rises up in the air, passing over the Taiwan Power Building; eyes follow its rise and fall as it is swept on, as it then heads south flying over the Xindian River, entering the mountainous area of Wuchong River after scaring a flock of pigeons, leading a hawk to take to the air to reconnoiter, but disliking the din and sighs of humans, beasts, and cockroaches in the bag, it quickly shuns them, ever alert.

The garbage bag continues to fly in the direction of Baigi Mountain, the red clouds write huge characters in the western sky.

FLYING TEARS

Empty mountain, no one in sight

Among dense bracken, a power saw roars, a squirrel barks in alarm on a high branch, a flying squirrel spreads its wings of flesh, a trembling masked civet races up a shaking tree trunk, the branches of the aloe and the uneven crowns of the trees are all waving with fear, trembling amid the roar of the power saw, time, one hundred years, three hundred years, one thousand years all become wood shavings dancing in the sky, time, one thousand years, two thousand years fall with a deafening roar. The past falls, the future falls.

Fresh green blood flows from the small crushed blades of grass.
Holding up a white feathered umbrella, traveling far to spread sadness
The dandelions are flying tears

OXALIS BOMB

An oxalis plant, escaping the bright autumn sun, is pulled up from the shade of the fern leaves by a rough hand, three hearts form one deep green leaf, small, pale purple flowers tinged slightly yellow. Do you want to taste the flavor of autumn? Sour? A little. Sweet? A little. Or place it on a breast that smells of milk. Where immediately it is pressed tightly, squeezed chest to chest, mouth sucking mouth, necks inset, the flowers and leaves flattened, the hammer-shaped pod ripens ever so gradually, warmed by the body heat of two people, and when the two bodies part, the pod pops open, not only with a shout of joy we cannot hear, but it also plants the tiny greenish-white seeds together with the slight sadness of autumn deep in the hearts of woman and man.

滅火機

憤怒昇起來的日午，家凝視着
墙上的滅火機，一個小孩走來對家
說：「看哪！你的眼睛裡有兩個滅
火機」為了這無邪的告白，捧
著他的雙頰，我不禁哭了。
我看見有兩個家分別在他眼中
流淚；他没有再告訴家，在秘那
些淚珠的鑑照中有多少個他自己。

民九三年秋於風馬驛

商禽

Fire Extinguisher
Shang Qin

Provided by National Museum of Taiwan Literature

電鎖　　　　商禽

這晚，我住的那一帶的路燈又準时
左午夜停電了。

當我在掏鑰匙的時候，好心的計程
司機趁倒車之便把車頭對準我
的身後，強烈的燈光將一個中
年人濃黑的身影　在留情的
投射在鐵門上，直到從一串鑰
匙中選出了正確的那一支對準
我心臟的部佐插進去，好心的計
程車司機才把車開走。

我也不終於插生我心臟中的鑰匙
輕輕的轉動一下，哎，隨即把這
段撬巧的金屬從心中拔出來順
勢一陣新然的走了進去。

没多久我便習慣了其中的黑暗。

Electric Lock
Shang Qin

Provided by National Museum of Taiwan Literature

CAMBRIA LITERATURE IN TAIWAN SERIES
General Editor: Nikky Lin
(National Taiwan Normal University)

The All-Seeing Eye: Collected Poems by Shang Qin, translated by John Balcom

A Taiwanese Literature Reader edited by Nikky Lin

The Soul of Jade Mountain by Husluman Vava, translated by Terence Russell

A History of Taiwan Literature by Ye Shitao, translated by Christopher Lupke

A Son of Taiwan: Stories of Government Atrocity edited by Howard Goldblatt and Sylvia Li-chun Lin

Transitions in Taiwan: Stories of the White Terror edited by Ian Rowen

Queer Taiwanese Literature: A Reader edited by Howard Chiang